Coloring Books for Adults

& Pa

MW01598442

© Susan Mowery

dream.relaxations@gmail.com

Twitter   @colorpagefree

Facebook   lifeescapescoloringbooks

# http://coloringbooksforadults.shop

## THIS IS A GRAYSCALE ADULT COLORING BOOK

Grayscale is very different than standard coloring books. It is designed for those who wish to create realistic colored images.

We have included coloring tips and instructions in the back of the book.

Visit http://coloringbooksforadults.shop for
• More great coloring books by various artists
• Examples of what's inside our coloring books
• Color guides or our grayscale coloring books
• How to color grayscale Instruction videos
• Free sample coloring pages to download
• Purchase digital versions of our coloring books
• Send us your colored pages for display

## for Inquiries not regarding artwork
### Contact Kimberly: life.escapes.series@gmail.com

# Preview

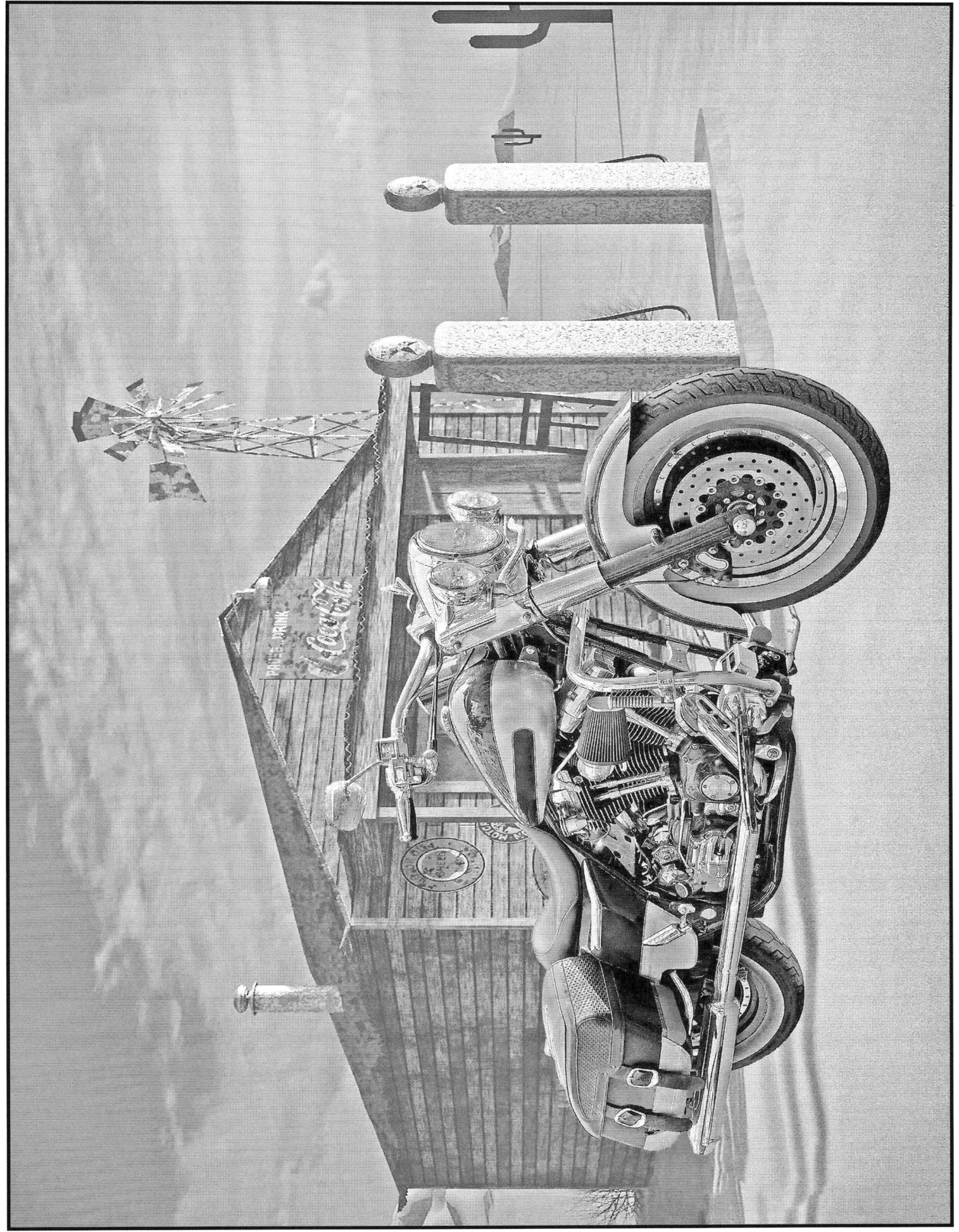

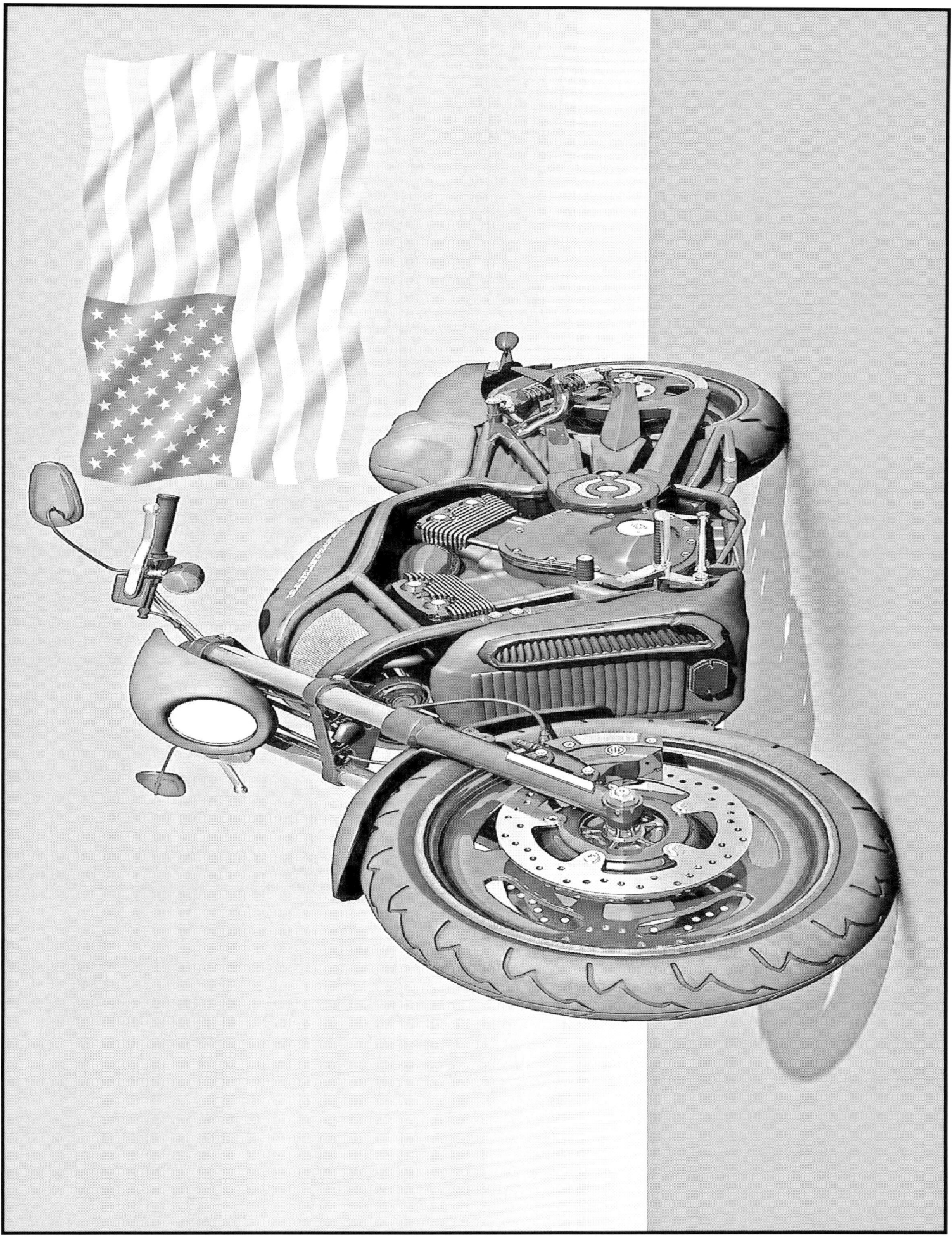

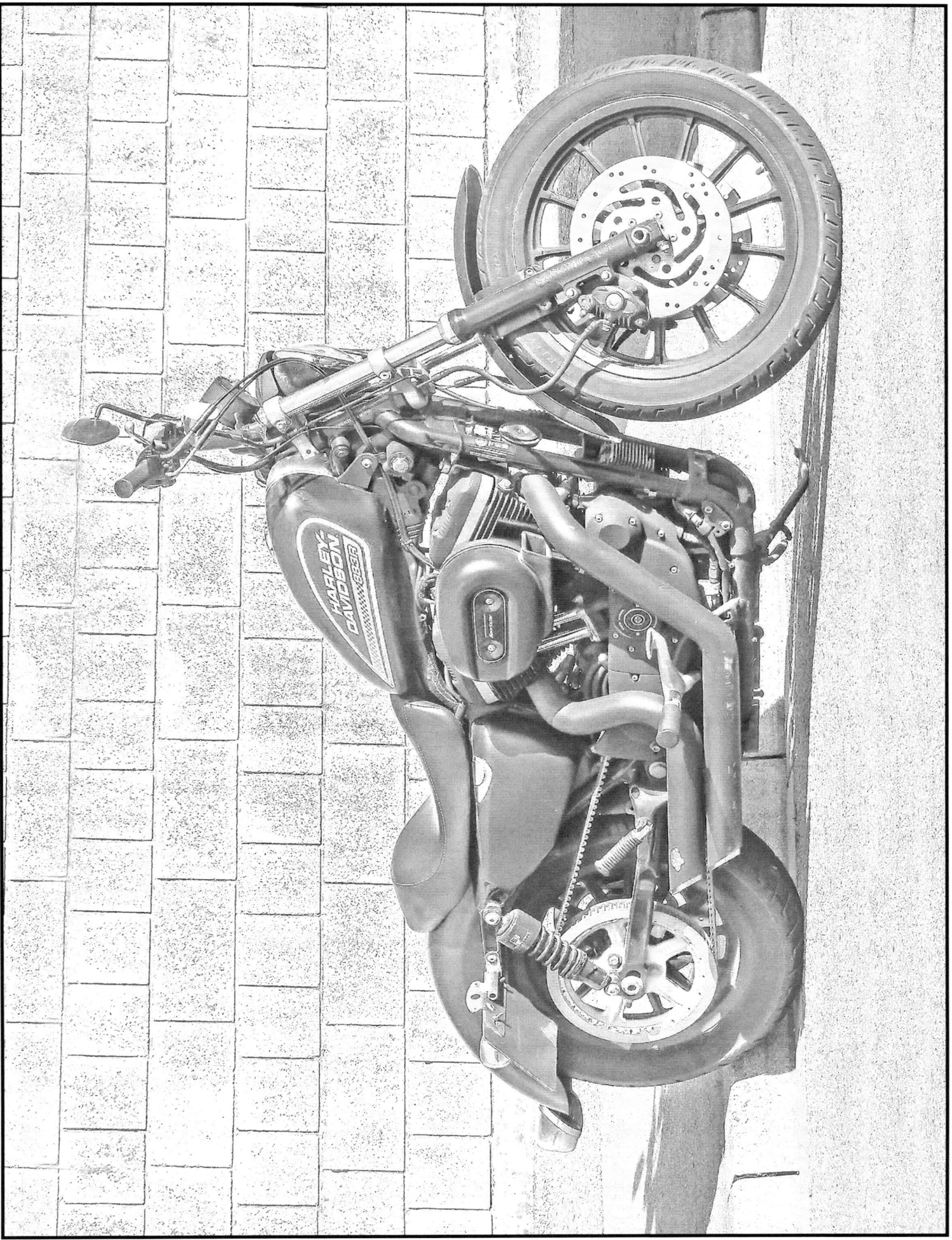

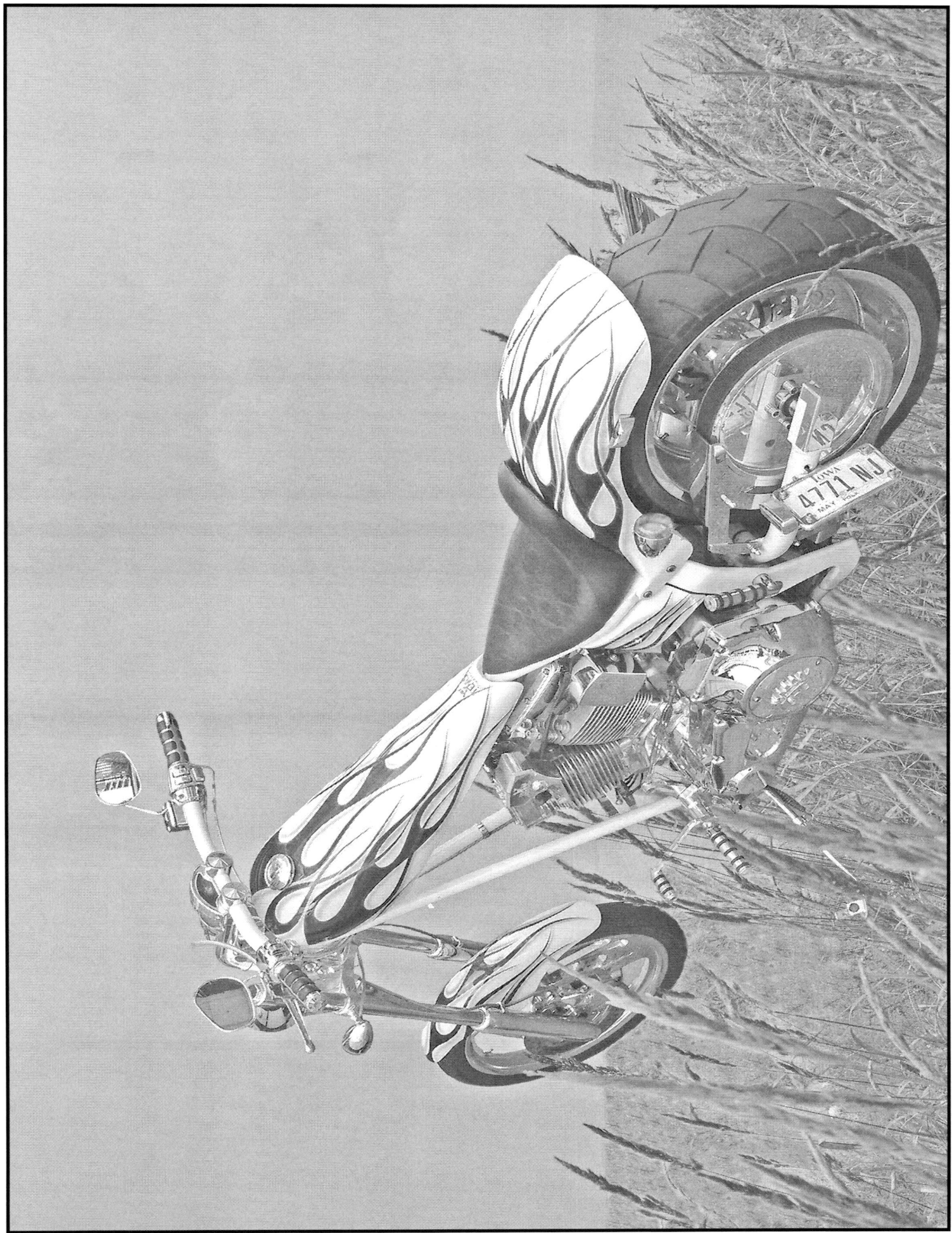

**http://coloringbooksforadults.shop**

pdf includes color guide

## HOW TO GET YOUR FREE DIGITAL COPY

1. locate one of the following
   Amazon order confirmation email
   Amazon delivery confirmation email
2. forward to life.escapes.series@gmail.com
   confirmation emails must show product

### OR

1. locate your invoice in your Amazon acct.
2. take a picture of, screenshot of or print and scan your invoice
3. send it to us at the email below or go to

http://coloringbooksforadults.shop/contact
to submit it via drag and drop form

then we will send you a download link

### Still Need Help?

life.escapes.series@gmail.com

# Tips for coloring grayscale images

1. We use a different method than other grayscale artists. Our method is light grayscale with enhanced detailing and texture. This is to assist beginning grayscale colorists. Advanced colorists find this method makes coloring realistically easier and faster.

2. Some animals and other objects were added to images. These may appear fake or obviously added. Once your image is colored, it will all blend together nicely and added objects will appear as though they belong.

3. Some areas in images may not be clearly defined, such as objects in distance. This is where you may use your imagination to color in or draw your own things right over the area. This is where grayscale comes in handy. Don't be afraid of what you can't make out, just change it to your liking.

4. Grayscale images turn out most realistic when using soft core colored pencils. Of course, you can use what you want but your results may not be as intended.

5. Even though our grayscale technique is a bit different than the standard, the coloring methods are the same. Watch video tutorials on coloring grayscale images on our website at http://coloringbooksforadults.shop

6. Grayscale helps you to identify where light, medium and dark coloring belong. Think of it as color by number, only without the numbers. Dark areas may indicate where a dark color should be use. This is often the case where shadows exist. Black areas typically indicate complete shadow where no light exists. This helps your images look as realistic as possible.

7. Some images in this book are easier to color than others. This is to provide for all skill levels and to be able to increase your skills as you go within one book.

# Basic Grayscale Coloring Instructions

Step 1 - Start in light areas with a light color foundation. It is not necessary to completely fill in the area. It should look and feel much like sketching.

Step 2 - Color over darker areas and texturing lines in that area with a darker color.

Step 3 - Color over the light area from step 1 with other or medium colors. For example, grass is not just green, it may contain brown and yellow as well as several shades of green. Soft core colored pencils make blending colors easier, which is why they are recommended for this coloring method.

Step 4 - Optional...blend all colors you've added to an area with a white colored pencil. This also help to add natural looking highlights.

Step 5 - Continue coloring the most clearly defined areas.

Step 6 - Once you have completed all clearly defined areas, you can now more easily see what should be in the not-so-clear areas. You may be able to continue with a color range such as a tree line. Or you may see fit to add something of your own to the image. This is to benefit your imagination and to improve upon your coloring skills. Just face your fear and go for it. You will be pleasantly surprised.

**We want you to enjoy your coloring experience**

**If you are struggling with an image, please go to http://coloringbooksforadults.shop to see all pages in this book in full color (if available). You will also find videos on how to color grayscale. If you still need assistance, please email Kimberly at life.escapes.series@gmail.com**

# COLOR TEST PAGE

# Adult Coloring Books
## http://coloringbooksforadults.shop
## life.escapes.series@gmail.com

You might also enjoy adult coloring books from our partnering artists

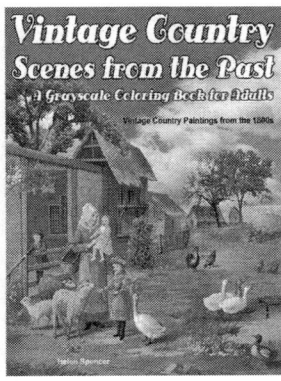

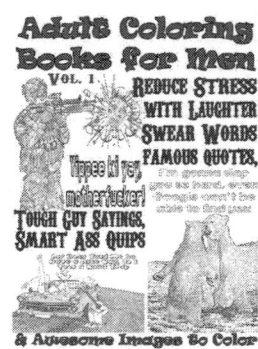

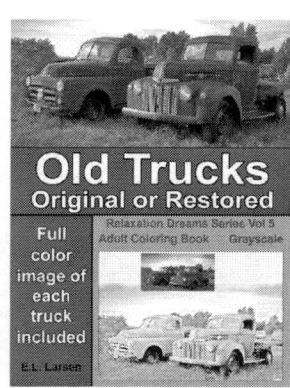

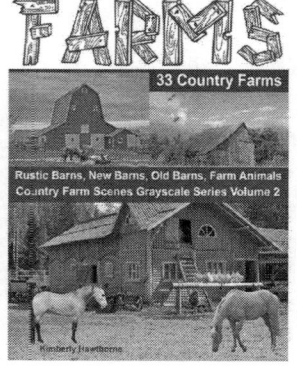

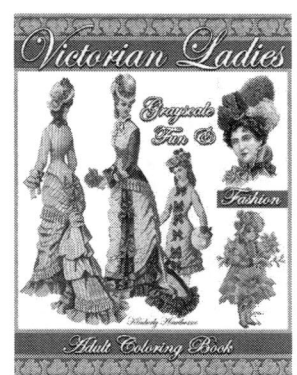

Manufactured by Amazon.ca
Bolton, ON